W9-DDM-050

2007

The Life and Work of
Mary Cassatt

Ernestine Giesecke

Heinemann Library
Chicago, Illinois

3 1267 13980 2985

© 2000, 2006 Heinemann Library
a division of Reed Elsevier Inc.
Chicago, Illinois

Customer Service 888-454-2279
Visit our website at www.heinemannraintree.com

All rights reserved. No part of this publication may be reproduced or transmitted in any form or by any means, electronic or mechanical, including photocopying, recording, taping, or any information storage and retrieval system, without permission in writing from the publisher.

Designed by Jo Malivoire and Q2A Creative
Printed in China by South China Printing Company

10 09 08 07 06
10 9 8 7 6 5 4 3 2 1

New edition ISBN: 1-40348-493-7 (hardcover)
                                  1-40348-504-6 (paperback)

The Library of Congress has cataloged the first edition as follows:
Giesecke, Ernestine, 1945-
                  Mary Cassatt / Ernestine Giesecke.
                              p. cm. — (The life and work of–) (Heinemann profiles)
                  Includes bibliographical references and index.
                  Summary: Introduces the life and work of Mary Cassatt, discussing
her early years, life in the United States and Paris, and
development as an artist.
                  ISBN 0 431 09883 2 (lib. bdg.)
                  1. Cassatt, Mary, 1844-1926 Juvenile literature. 2. Artists-
-United States Biography Juvenile literature. [1. Cassatt, Mary,
1844-1926. 2. Artists 3. Women Biography. 4. Painting, American.
5. Art appreciation] I. Title. II. Series. III. Series:
Heinemann profiles.
N6537.C35G54 1999
759. 13—dc21   99-14557
[B]   CIP

Acknowledgments
The author and publishers are grateful to the following for permission to reproduce copyright material:
The Pennsylvania Academy of Fine Arts, Philadelphia, pp. 4, 8; The Denver Art Museum, Anonymous Bequest, p. 5; Drawing of Cassatt Family, Peter Baumgartner, 1854, Anonymous Owner, p. 6; Fine Arts Museums of San Francisco, Museum purchase, William H. Nobel Bequest Fund, 1979.35, p. 7; Founders Society Purchase, Robert H. Tannahill Foundation Fund, The Detroit Institute of Arts, p. 9; Corbis/Bettmann, p. 10; The Roland P. Murdock Collection, Wichita Art Museum, Wichita, Kansas, p.11; Bibliotheque Nationale, Department des Estampes, p. 12; Philadelphia Museum of Art, W.P. Wilstach Collection, p. 13; Erich Lessing/Art Resource, p. 14; Sterling and Francine Clark Art Institute, p. 15; The Bridgeman Art Library International, Ltd., pp. 16, 23; Collection of Mr. and Mrs. Paul Mellon, ©1999 Board of Trustees, National Gallery of Art, Washington, 1878, p.17; National Portrait Gallery, Smithsonian Institution. Gift of the Morris and Gwendolyn Cafritz Foundation and the Regents' Major Acquisitions fund, Smithsonian Institution, p. 18; The Metropolitan Museum of Art, Bequest of Edith H. Proskauer, 1975, p. 19; Anonymous Gift in Honor of Eugenia Cassatt Madeira

Cover photograph: *Self Portrait* by Mary Cassatt, reproduced with permission of the National Portrait Gallery, Smithsonian Institution / Art Resource, NY.

The publishers would like to thank Nancy Harris for her assistance in the preparation of this book.

Every effort has been made to contact copyright holders of any material reproduced in this book. Any omissions will be rectified in subsequent printings if notice is given to the publisher.

The paper used to print this book comes from sustainable sources.

Some words in this book are in bold, **like this.** You can find out what they mean by looking in the Glossary.

Contents

Who was Mary Cassatt?

Mary Cassatt was an American artist. She was a successful woman painter. This was at a time when most painters were men.

Most of Mary's art shows **scenes** from everyday life. Some of her most well-known paintings are of mothers and children.

Early Years

Mary was born on May 22 1844 in Pittsburgh, Pennsylvania. When Mary was seven years old she moved to Paris in France with her family. Later they moved to Germany. Mary was 10 when this picture was drawn.

At school Mary **studied** many subjects. She liked drawing and music. When Mary became an artist, she painted **portraits** of her family. This portrait shows her mother, Katherine Cassatt.

Philadelphia Art Student

In 1855 Mary and her family moved back to the United States. When Mary was 17 years old she went to the Pennsylvania Academy of Fine Arts. Mary is the girl on the right of the picture.

Mary learned to draw from life and by **studying** other works of art. She liked to ride horses with her older brother, Alexander. This is a **portrait** Mary painted of him when she was older.

Paris Art Student

When Mary was 21 years old, she traveled to Paris. She wanted to learn about art. She **studied** works of art by great artists. She copied paintings in a museum called the Louvre.

Mary studied **Madonna and Child** paintings. This helped her to paint her own pictures of mothers caring for their small children, such as this one.

The Salon

In 1868 when Mary was 24 years old, her work was chosen to be shown in the **Salon** in Paris. The Salon was a place where artists whose paintings were selected showed their work.

This painting is called *On the Balcony During Carnival*. It is like many of the paintings Mary made when she first moved to Paris. It is the type of painting the Salon **judges** liked.

Professional Artist

Mary **exhibited** in the **Salon** for a few more years. But she grew tired of having to paint what would please the **judges** at the Salon.

Mary did not want to paint **models** anymore. She did not want to use dark colors like in this painting. She wanted to paint things as she saw them.

Changing Her Ways

In 1877 Mary met the artist Edgar Degas. Edgar introduced Mary to other painters. These painters were known as the **Impressionists**. The Impressionists painted **scenes** of everyday life.

The Impressionists painted with **splotches** of color. Mary liked the colors they used and the way they used them. She made this painting soon after she met Edgar.

Joining the Impressionists

Mary and Edgar became good friends. They visited each other's **studios**. They talked about their work. They gave each other ideas. Edgar Degas painted this **portrait** of Mary.

Mary used some of the **Impressionists'** ideas in her own paintings. She did this self-portrait in 1878. She used lighter colors and looser **brush strokes**.

Painting Real Life

Many **Impressionists** painted outdoor **scenes**. Mary used the Impressionist ideas, but she painted indoor scenes. The paintings tell us about Mary's life.

Most of Mary's paintings are **portraits** of her family, friends, and neighbors. Many things in Mary's paintings belonged to her. Look at the silver tea set on page 20. You can see it in the painting on this page.

Painting Women

Mary lived in a lively part of Paris near this café. Painters, musicians, and writers met at cafés to talk about their ideas. Mary and the women she knew read newspapers.

Mary sometimes painted women reading newspapers. This was something new in painting. At that time most artists painted **models** who **posed** just for the painting.

Mothers and Children

Mary never married or had any children. Mary's brother, Alexander, and his family stayed with her when they visited Europe. Mary loved her nieces and nephews. She often painted pictures of them.

Mary spent hours on each drawing and painting. Yet much of her work shows **scenes** that would be over very quickly. This is a painting of a mother washing her sleepy child.

French Countryside

Mary bought a house near Paris. She spent most of her time there. Her **studio** was on the second floor of her home. She could look out on to her pond and gardens.

This picture of ducks was **inspired** by the pond behind Mary's home. This picture is a print. A print allows an artist to make many copies of the same picture. Mary became very good at making prints.

A Lasting Impression

During the last years of Mary's life, her eyesight failed. She could not paint. Mary Cassatt died on June 14 1926. She was 82 years old.

People still remember Mary Cassatt for her gentle pictures of mothers and children. She was important as a female artist because she was the only American to exhibit with the Impressionists.

Timeline

1844	Mary Cassatt is born on May 22 in Pittsburgh, Pennsylvania.
1861	Mary begins her studies at the Pennsylvania Academy of Fine Arts, Philadelphia.
1865–70	Mary travels in Europe.
1868	Mary's work is first **exhibited** at the **Salon**.
1879	Mary exhibits with the **Impressionists**.
1893	Mary's first one-woman exhibition.
1900	World's Fair in Paris, France.
1914–18	World War I. Mary moves to Italy to avoid the war.
1926	Mary Cassatt dies on June 14.

Glossary

brush strokes marks left by an artist's paint brush

exhibit to show art in public

Impressionists group of artists who painted freely, showing light and movement

inspire to influence or guide

judge person who chose which pictures would be shown in the Salon

Madonna and Child work of art that shows Mary and baby Jesus

model person an artist paints or draws

portrait painting, drawing, or photograph of a person

pose to sit or stand while being drawn by an artist

Salon place in Paris where artists were invited to show their artwork

scene place or area

splotch large spot

studio place where an artist works

study to learn about a subject

More Books to Read

Wolfe, Gillian. *Oxford First Book of Art.* New York: OUP, 2004.

Raimondo, Joyce. *Picture This! Activities and Adventures in Impressionism.* New York: Watson-Guptill Publications Inc, 2004.

Woodhouse, Jayne. *The Life and Work of Edward Degas.* Chicago: Heinemann Library, 2002.

More Paintings to See

The Letter, 1890-91. National Gallery of Art, Washington, D.C., and Chicago Art Institute, Chicago, Il.

Sleepy Baby, 1910. Dallas Museum of Fine Art, Dallas, Tex.

Girl Brushing Her Hair, 1886. Metropolitan Museum of Art, New York, N.Y.

Index